*hi Natali
what do you
to someone so freaking
awesome? im thankful that
i have the privilege of calling
you my friend !! i love you!
♡ greg*

inspired by and dedicated to
Jesus and all the the soulfully beautiful
people in my life

1

index

growth
and
change

endings, beginnings, and all that's in between
—

there's redemption
resounding in everything

slow, under-the-surface growth
is every bit as valuable as the growth that
everyone can see

here is where the unimportant
melts away
and what is true gold
emerges in the light
of a new day

this new chapter
will be a fresh beginning
even your brokenness will be redeemed
in deepened healing
because maybe there were things that had to break
for you to really heal

this new chapter
will be one of deepened faith
through the middle of the shockwaves
of the very things that threatened to tear you apart
because this is a new chapter

here is where i find Him
because here's where He found me
in the middle i've found grace
because in the middle i learned to see
nearer than my heartbeat,
in every breath i breathe.
Jesus i'm learning
to see You in everything.

from gray to vibrant
from winter to spring
in the middle of change
You remind me how to breathe

your courage is growing
soon it will tower high above all your worry
your courage is growing
and when courage grows in you
it grows in people around you too
your courage is growing
because your faith is growing too

don't water bitterness
and then expect peace
to grow

just when i thought i had left a mountaintop
to travel an endless valley
i reached a new peak
and You showed me there was an endless
stretch of more as far as my eyes could see

maybe there are things You are growing me to be
that never would be possible
in the safety of familiarity

i guess words are just our way of bottling
up moments and feelings so that we can
always keep them with us

but sometimes the feelings and moments
are too big to fit in our little bottles

and instead they become a part of us

but maybe there are things buried in your soul
just waiting to be watered
so they have a chance to grow

spring smells like a fresh start,
when the layers built up during the winter
are peeled away
and we're left bare and raw—
it's a shedding of the things that clung to
our souls,
leaving us free
to allow fresh spring rain to wash away
the things that block the light from reaching
our souls,
to find newness in the friendly smell of
soft, rich soil,
to absorb the sunlight and find rest in its
silent strength—
spring is redemption,
it's meaning and life emerging out of the
long, cold winter
and spring always comes

newness
God is awakening our souls
it's not reverting to the way things were
it's redemption resonating in everything
it's innocence and truth deepening
through the very things that almost broke them
it's night turning to day, shadow turning to light
placed into the hands of a God who makes sense out
of messes
not by fixing them to fit our concept of
"okay"
but by illuminating them in such a way that
makes it all a part of something meaningful in the
light of His grace
He's bringing newness
it's not restoring of something old
it's recreating
it's everything being undone and remade
it's the growth and deepening of our souls,
us becoming the truest versions of
ourselves
in the hands of the One who most fully
knows us and who we're meant to be

but the sun still rose
the birds still sang
and i realized everything
would be okay

it's difficult
it will challenge you,
stretch you,
push you to new heights you didn't feel
capable of reaching
it's hard,
but what if it's hard because it's
something worthwhile?

i know the road is long
and sometimes you can't remember what
your destination looks like
i know there's a lot that doesn't make
sense
and it feels like you stumble and trip
with every step
but more than anything, i know
that no matter what, you never walk this
road alone

but when the wind blew strong

the tree sunk its roots deeper

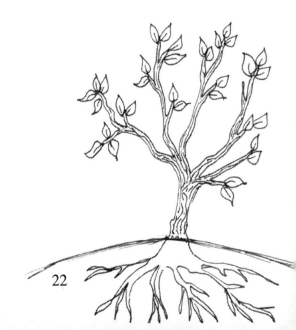

the funny thing about breakthroughs is that
sometimes i think
there are a lot of things you have to go
through
and parts of you that have to break
before you emerge into the relief and peace of finding
meaning in all of it

moments pass
memories fade
but somewhere in my heart
they always stay
in the way i talk
the way i breathe
the way i walk
the way i see
a million miles and moments away,
but in a million ways they still remain

i used to open my hands for the sweet
and clench them up tight against the bitter,
but i'm learning to see
God brings just as much meaning through
lemons
as through honey
i don't want the pleasantness of the easy
without the richness of the difficult
because it's in the raw and the mess
that we grow and learn,
deepen, develop
we were never meant to live life comfortably
numb

everything was changing
i felt like i was breaking
but what i thought would shatter my soul
is what God used to make me whole
the things that were uncomfortable
are the things that taught me how to grow

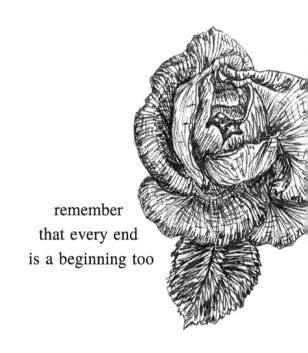

remember
that every end
is a beginning too

there are no
shortcuts to the places
most worth going

but if i hadn't been buried
i might have never grown
and maybe it's a greater tragedy to live stuck
inside a shell, never quite alive
than to go through the night and emerge
into the fullness of a fresh warm day

because sometimes the things that break us
can bring about the most beautiful beginnings of all

and when i hold everything up to the light
i can see
that nothing is wasted when God is
the gardener of our souls

in deep darkness
your soul can still find deep light
the places that feel the blackest will
be the ones that can hold the most light
through the night everything will be alright
you will emerge
incandescent

what you water in your life
is what will grow in your life

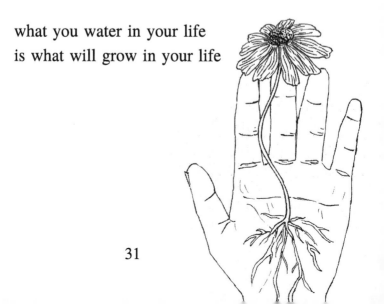

for the things i've lost
and the things i've found
for what i've left behind
and what i've gained
in all i've done right
and in all the times i've failed
in all i've learned
and in all i still don't understand
let me know
there's grace
grace that will be steady
unchanging
constant within me
still with me
in
everything

there's no place Your grace won't hold me,
and there's no place Your peace won't reach.
in every season of my story,
where You are is home to me

sow light
grow bright
even when it's night
keep on holding tight
to the good and right
and keep sowing light

but the rains that brought us the overcast days
brought us new life too

it's okay that you're not there yet
none of us are
it's okay that the growth looks
messy and raw and real
it's okay that the progress is slow
and that you don't have all the answers

you don't have to wait for the final product to breathe
grace is less about making it to the finish line first
and more about learning to keep breathing along the way
in the in-between moments

it's okay that you're unfinished

and here
with the sun breaking through the clouds
and beautiful growth pushing itself to the surface of the
soil,
your soul is being resurrected

it's not an altering of who you're meant to be—
it's an awakening of new life,
illuminating the parts of you that have been there all along
just waiting to meet the sun so they have a chance to grow

seeds you've long forgotten about
and long given up on
are breathing with life
and shooting up towards the sky

feel your purpose being gently renewed
breathe in deep the fresh spring scent of
resurrection

growth isn't an event —
its a process

in the middle of tremendous darkness
is where God is preparing your soul
for tremendous light

somewhere along the way
your courage grew so great
that it was something
comfort zones couldn't contain

peace beckons you towards a sunlit field
where sweet, unrushed things grow

sometimes the sun sets and rises again
as God's way of awakening inside of us
colors we didn't realize were there

becoming

who we are,
who we're becoming,
and who we're meant
to be

though the world is loud,

quiet your soul

we've learned to walk past golden sunsets and step
over glittering puddles,
look unaffectedly into eyes that speak wordless,
soulful poetry
and step around soft puppies with happy tails
as if this miracle of a life is unremarkable and
commonplace

we've learned to see without really seeing

it does matter
what you fill your mind with
what you surround yourself with
what you feed your soul with

the person you become tomorrow
starts with the decisions you make today
it does matter

i hope that even when their words are ones
that bite and sting,
you don't let their opinions crowd out the light

i hope you stay strong,
but more than anything,
i hope you are sure of who you are meant to be
no matter what the rest of the world sees

don't fill yourself
with things that will leave you emptier

maybe this can be the season where you
discover what parts of you are really you
apart from all of the things that have
clung to you from the world around you

maybe this is the season where all the
confusion in your mind can find its way to a
place of stillness

and through the chaos of all that you are
and all that the world tells you to be,
you can hear the sure, peaceful whisper
of God telling you what He sees in you

i don't just trip through
my eyes see, i breathe, fully here,
i am flourishing

you're defined by all the things God says you are,

not by the things they say you aren't

even when the world feels so cold,
don't let your heart go numb—
your strength will not be found in building
up layers of protection,
but in letting the fire in your soul thaw the
frost around you

what's going on around you
doesn't have to dictate
what happens inside of you—
your surroundings don't have to determine
the posture of your heart

i just hope you know today
that no matter what yesterday looked like
and no matter what happens tomorrow,
no matter what people say or don't say
about you
you are more than the things you don't
understand
you are more than the decisions you've
made
you are more than your mistakes and
you are more than just the sum of your
good days and bad days

and when God looks at you that more is
what He sees
He sees who you're becoming
He sees your personality, your hopes,
your dreams, your uncertainties, and everything
in between
you are more

change the world
but don't wait until you have what it takes
don't wait on funding
don't wait on people's opinions
don't wait on the perfect idea
but most importantly,
don't wait until you're ready
because the secret to changing the world is—
start
start small
start now
start living out the change that you want to see
start with what you do know even when
there are a million things you don't know

i see you in the corner
you've forgotten how to breathe
around you so much hustle
you can't remember how to be
you're told your worth is in the loudness
of the echo your life leaves
as if it doesn't even matter
what words your voice is saying
but here can be the place
you remember how to breathe
remember who you are
apart from what they see

uncertainties
heart racing
hands shaking
fears are choking confidence
how do i get over this?
the world is so loud
that i can't hear a thing
i suck air in
ease it out
everything is quiet now
here in the still
i hear Your heart
i find my voice
i was never meant
to live under the pressure of all the world's noise
here in the stillness i remember who i am
in stillness is where You give me strength to stand

but what if we were different?
what if we gave—
not to receive something in return,
but because of all that's been given to us?

what if we spoke—
not just to be heard above all the noise,
but because we had words worth saying?

what if we were kind—
not so that people will be kind back to us,
but because kindness is just naturally a part
of our character?
what if we were different?

let your skin be thick
your heart be soft
and your mind be sharp

you can choose

to be respectful even when you're
disrespected,
to listen patiently even when your voice
has been ignored,
to love even when your love is repaid
with hate,
to forgive even when others refuse to
forgive,
to respond maturely to immaturity,
to give even when everyone else does
nothing but take

you don't have to live by the world's
rules
you can choose

i find my strength in being still
when over all the world's noise,
i hear Your whisper

here is where i'm made whole,
because i am most fully myself
when i am wholly and completely Yours

my heart finds strength in stillness
because no matter what
You're still here

somehow the sun rises every day
i wonder where she gets the strength
every night i watch her leave
and wonder if i'm quite naive
to trust she will be back again
and believe tomorrow will begin

i wonder if the sun gets tired
when her outside glow
is the sole reason she's admired,
when they only love her on sunny days
and don't bother getting to know
the heart behind her rays

somehow the sun rises everyday
and for that i think she's very brave
even when she's taken for granted
her light is never
quenched or dampened

she doesn't need attention
or ask for recognition
because she knows her beauty could never
be changed
by the things that people do or say

the darkness isn't as scary

once you carry the light
inside you

if only we realized that we don't have to
let the darkness dull our light—
if only we realized that if we let it, this
light within us could shatter the darkness

i really don't think strength is fighting the hardest
or shouting the loudest—
strength is finding your peace in the
middle of a chaotic world

my prayer for you today is that you are
uncomfortable,
that your convictions are stronger than
your complacency,
that your heart doesn't run from the hard things,
that you choose what is healthy, not what is easy,
that you do what is right, not what is
convenient,
that your passion outweighs your
uncertainties,
and that your faith is too great to let you live
a conventional and comfortable life

sometimes we become so accustomed to words
that represent things
that we lose sight of the uncontainable,
inexpressible fullness
of the essence of the things themselves

we don't always need words to hold our moments
and feelings
because sometimes they're too big for words
anyways
it's okay to be left speechless

but you get to choose which things roll like raindrops
off of an umbrella
and which things stick to you and
determine who you become

you aren't worth any more on the days when they notice you
notice you
or any less on the days when they don't

existing
was never meant to be a competition
you can live and grow and learn
without living under the pressure of
some manufactured concept of
"good enough"

i know you thought that time would fix
everything
but all time did was fix your perspective
until you were ready to start fixing what you
could for yourself and others

let's spend more
time working, towards
a fulfilling reality, than
a successful appearance

what would happen if we cared more
about growing into the best version of
ourselves than about looking finished?

we've become so obsessed with the idea
of success and recognition
that we've stopped really caring what it is
that we succeed at
and what we're remembered for
but what if our goal was growing into
who we're made to be
instead of becoming the person they're
most ready to shine a spotlight on?

sometimes people become
what we tell them they can be
and treat them like they already are

our problem was never that we loved people too much—
but rather that we confused love with dependency
and learned to equate the sum of our worth with the sum of
their acceptance—
our problem was never that we loved too much

the way we live
will always speak
louder than the
words we say

what if we decided to not let people's opinions
determine who we become,

and stopped letting our fears turn into excuses?

what if we cared more about being kind than
about being cool,

and learned to disagree with each other without
hurting and hating each other?

what if we built each other up instead of
tearing each other down,

and spoke more loudly about what we are
for than about what we are against?

what if we stopped waiting for things to be
different, and started making a difference?

when we live our lives to prove ourselves to people,
we trade purpose for approval

grace
and
truth

grace that calms the storm within us

—

truth that anchors our souls to the shore

there's something
about seeing Your
love that changes
the way i see
everything else

though your uncertainties seem colossal
they will crumble when met by grace
and the light will come flooding in
and fill the empty space

let this be where the light finds you
where the sour and bitter
are met with redeeming sweet

let this be where the light finds you
where in a world that once seemed dull
you see color in everything

let this be where the light finds you
where the golden glow of sunlight
rips through the shadows surrounding you

let this be where the light finds you
where love radically changes
who you are and the way you see

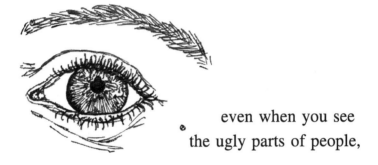

even when you see
the ugly parts of people,

don't stop looking for the beautiful

the truth that cuts,
the grace that heals—
we need them both

grace isn't something you have to look far to find

you can reach out a hand and touch it no matter
where you are— with every breath we can know
God more fully, directly, and personally than our
body know and abides in the oxygen in our lungs

breathing in the atmosphere of His presentness,
His grace becomes ingrained in the very fibers of
our being

like most important
things in life,
loving isn't easy,
but it is simple

come to the light
open your hands
find wholeness, find rest
find strength to stand

come to the light
find what is true
there's grace that can hold you
all the way through

come to the light
come and receive
there is peace that is steady
that never will leave

come to the light
when you feel all alone
you're seen and you're chosen
never too far from home

when it's right
you won't have to chase it down
make it stay
or change yourself to find it
when it's right you won't have to stretch yourself thin
trying to justify it
you won't have to worry about it
when it's right God will send it to you
it will fit with who you are
and who God is growing you to be

sometimes Jesus calms
the storm,
but sometimes He teaches
you to walk on the waves
instead

i think you'll find
that being kind usually benefits you
more than it costs you

sometimes God leads us with a gentle whisper

because the real treasure is found not just in the
words He is saying,

but in the closeness required to hear His voice

You looked at me
and saw the things i couldn't see
You looked at me
and spoke light into life in me

we become distressed and disappointed
when we need a break
but it's okay
to be tired
just find rest in the
right
places

the wind is loud
the waves are fierce
my whole world is shaking
then You appear
who knew that one word
could eclipse all my fear
but You say "come"
and all i see is You near
everything else seems small
the noise disappears
i step onto the waves
all is well, You are here

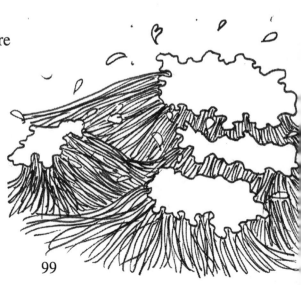

the things you
allow to build you
up are the things
that have the
power to tear you
down too

when you've known what it's like
to recognize
a pain you've felt
in another's eyes
then you've known what it's like
to empathize

we chase things that make us feel deeply
and crave things that make us feel alive,
but with You
in every breath
i am deeply alive
You give me everything i need

your flame shivered
but didn't go out
in the dark of night
grace abounds

your eyes voice the murmurs of your soul,
telling me the things your words can't say
there are a hundred things i would let you know,
but words can't make it all okay
i just hope you know you're heard
right here, right now
you are safe
i wish that i could heal your hurt,
but i'll do what i can, i'll be here
i'll stay

this beauty is
breathtaking —
like nothing i've ever
seen

this beauty is
breathtaking —
but for the first time i
really breathe

You breathe colors
every word You speak is art
and here my heart resounds with the
things You've said i can be
and i see You making art out of me

maybe we can let the things that make us trip
and falter
be the things that teach us to lean into Jesus for strength

shadows tall
in the light they fall
it's so complex, but simple too
but now i find myself alive here with You
one thing i know that is for sure
You're the more we were always looking for

more and more i see
it's not what i accomplish,
but me that You love

when we ask for the sweet without the bitter
we risk ending up with a life coldly and
comfortably devoid of both

feel deeply
but bring those deep feelings and hold them
in the light
so that you don't live blindly driven
by waves of emotion inside you that you don't
fully understand
but instead live in the clarity that the light
brings

you

inspired by the stunning and soulful
people in my life

you're stunning—
not the kind of stunning that you put in a picture frame and
hang on your wall,
but the kind of stunning that is so far beyond your outer
beauty that no picture could ever capture it

you're the kind of stunning that is evident in the soul beauty
ingrained in you eyes, in your ideas, in your words, and in
the way you live

you are not the kind of stunning that people admire and
envy and then quickly forget—
you are the kind of stunning that shines from the inside out,
illuminating the beauty in others too

you are the kind of stunning that sends perpetual echoes of
grace and truth resonating through people's lives even when
you're long gone

you aren't the kind of stunning that the world idealizes,
but you are the kind of stunning that the world needs

you're a fighter
not fighting your way to the top
but fighting for the people that have been pushed to the bottom

you're a fighter
not fighting to get ahead
but fighting for the people that have lost the will to fight for
themselves

you're a fighter
not fighting for admiration
but for transformation

you're a fighter
of fierce, courageous kindness
and that's the bravest kind of fighter of all

kind soul,
i think it's brave that in a hard world
you've remained soft,
that when you're surrounded by cold,
you radiate warmth

in a world where everything can seem so
complicated,
you are simply you
in the most beautiful way possible

and i think that's brave

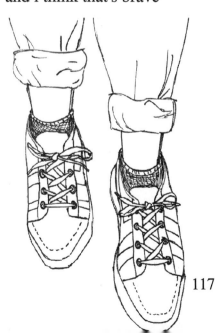

you're a living, breathing promise made by God
on its way to being fulfilled
your journey is held by faithfulness
more concrete than anything you could have built

you look at darkness
and instead of
being pulled into its
gravity
you speak light

i see a spark of freedom in your eyes—

you used to worry about not fitting in
but now you're more worried about fitting in
in the wrong places
now you know who you are
and you know who you're not
and that's beautiful

i know you've seen a lot of things
that have colored who you are
i know you've been so many places
that have left you rough and scarred
but you're still you
even when it's hard to see
in your heart is buried still
the truth of who you're made to be

redemption can find you right in this spot
in between all you are
and all you're not
you can be found, you're not too far
for good things to find a way to your heart

they tell you to chase the rain

but your soul was made for oceans

the world was cold today
you're a ray of sun
that came my way
the harsh wind tried
to push you away
but through it all you were here,
you stayed

the world was cold today,
but the sun sent you
now i'm okay
the harsh wind colored
the whole world gray
but my soul is bright because
you stayed

when i'm with you i feel your soul—
i feel the essence of who you are
pulsating behind every part of you,
the breath behind your words,
the heartbeat behind your every action

when i'm with you i feel your soul—
wildly full of potential beyond what you
can imagine
i can see your personality coloring the
atmosphere around you,
reflecting something beautiful inside you
that can't be seen,
but that is so obvious

there's something magnetic and contagious
about heartfelt kindness
—

you live sweetness from a soul of honey
and now i feel something inside me
awakened to love better and sweeter

your freedom brings me closer to freedom
your love brings me closer to love
in your eyes i glimpse liberating truth
and with every word you speak, i feel
Jesus here in you

you were never meant to adjust to the
rhythm of the world around you
no matter what song the world is playing
your heart keeps beating to its
own beautiful beat

the words you say
are an echo of the song
your soul is singing

resilient
no matter how many times you were battered and
beaten
you rose
you rose above the shadowy depths of bitterness
and met outer darkness with inner light

even in the middle of everything around you that was

so crooked and tangled
you stayed true
and refused to respond to hate with more hate
you rose above
not by pushing others down
but by building them up

in your kindness
i see resilience

who said you had to look like everyone else,
sound like everyone else,
and act like everyone else
to be beautiful?
your unruly freckles,
the way your ears turn red when you're nervous,
your loud laugh,
the way you always take the time to talk to kids,
the way you raise your eyebrows when you
fix your glasses on the bridge of your nose,
your eyes that are a hundred different shades of blue,
the little baby strands of hair that are
always out of place on your forehead,
the way you tilt your head to the side
when you're thinking—
the little things that make you you
are your own kind of beautiful, too

you don't look perfect
you look genuinely you
effortlessly beautiful
you look real
and real takes so much more bravery
than perfect

i see in you fresh beginnings—
raindrops on roses
birds singing on telephone wires
the sun breaking through the clouds
new nights and new days
your story doesn't end this way

you're not amazing because you're perfect

you're amazing because of the way you love
and live so beautifully despite your
imperfections

no amount of bitter
can silence your sweetness

you are an atmosphere shifter

there's a honey-golden glow
in the depths of your soul
that illuminates the room when you walk in

there's something in the way you laugh,
a sweet wisdom in the words you say--
there's something bright and fresh and
freeing about the scent you leave in the air

in a million ways the unaltered, incomparable
essence of who Jesus has grown you to be
sparks something in the people around you

you are an atmosphere shifter

so many people strive to be beautiful,

but the most beautiful people i know
are beautiful because of their ability to look past the ugly
and speak out the beauty they see in every
person, place, and situation they encounter

you've seen so many places full of darkness
you've found so much brokenness that you couldn't fix
but all the parts of your journey
that felt like they amounted to nothing
have led you here to this
now you can look back and see
God was bringing peace through everything
even when all you could see was darkness
you were leaving a little light everywhere you went

maybe you don't fit in
because your soul reaches for things
high up among the clouds
and you're not ready to settle for the things everyone
around you seems to want

maybe you don't fit in
because they tell you to be a daisy,
but you've been a sunflower all along

they call your kindness naive
but when i look at you i see strength
you don't love because you've never been hurt
but because you have—
you love because you've been betrayed
and instead of learning bitterness
you learned grace
and that, my friend, is strength

somehow in the middle of an uncertain, unstable world
you stayed true
that's not boring
that's steadfast, courageous might

even when there was nobody around to watch
you still shone just as brightly
because your light isn't an act
it's at the heart of who you are

to the kaleidoscopes in a colorblind world,

your beauty does not change depending
on whether or not people recognize it

i ask you how you leave fingerprints of grace
on all you see

you smile and say, "Jesus left fingerprints of grace
all over me"

you won't absorb the
shade they throw
'cause you're already
full of that golden
glow

your passion ignited
and burnt your worries to the ground
there are no shadows anymore
only light is standing now

you still smile
as the pain tears by
when they cut your wings
and ask you why
you haven't found
the strength to fly

you're the bravest kind of beautiful--
like soft clouds in the sky,
there's kindness in your face
even when you cry

love will find your soul
and fill the empty space
your broken parts
will find their place
because your soul is welcome
in the arms of grace

in you i see the snow of winter
and the bright of spring
fall and summer
and everything in between
because you've seen it all
and you're still ever-green

you don't have to prove a thing
let your soul breathe
the moments when you're trying the least to be something
you're not
are the moments you're closest to who you're meant to be
and those moments are beautiful

i think it's breathtaking
the way you know who you are
and with a life that speaks grace and truth
you empower other people to know who they are too

you don't have to change
yourself to fit into the
world's conceptualization
of beauty

because extraordinary
beauty can't be confined
to an ordinary standard

in the essence of your spirit
now peace is what i see
even through everything that changes
your heart's unrest has ceased
because you found something
that has stirred deep inside your soul
you found contentment
you found a God that makes you whole